THE JUBILEE ANOINTING
Marked for <u>Your</u> Miracle!

THE JUBILEE ANOINTING
Marked for <u>Your</u> Miracle!

By
Rod Parsley

RESULTS
PUBLISHING

ISBN: 1-880244-42-X
Copyright © 1998 by Rod Parsley.

Published by:
Results Publishing
Box 32903
Columbus, Ohio 43232-0903 USA

DEDICATION

This book is lovingly dedicated to the multitude of the saints of God — past, present and future. It is devoted to the young and old, small and great, powerful and prayerful, mighty and meek. It is written for every praying parent and grandparent. Its pages have been penned for every minister of the Gospel who has ever spent a myriad of sleepless nights travailing before the throne of God.

It is for those who will not be denied their position, delayed in their pursuit or detoured on their pathway to take the message of salvation, healing and deliverance, with signs and wonders following, to this generation.

It is for all those who have bowed their head, kissed the scepter of our Canaan King, Jesus Christ, and accepted the *"mark"* of His anointing as an eternal bond servant; and, in the words of the Son of God, Himself, will say:

The Spirit of the Lord [is] upon Me, because He has <u>anointed</u> Me [the Anointed One, the Messiah] to preach the good news (the Gospel) to the poor; He has sent Me to announce release to the captives and recovery of sight to the blind, to send forth as delivered those who are oppressed [who are downtrodden, bruised, crushed, and broken down by calamity], to proclaim the accepted and acceptable year of the Lord [the day when salvation and the free favors of God profusely abound] (Luke 4:18,19 AMP).

CONTENTS

Introduction

Bearing His Mark

Standing on the coasts of Caesarea Philippi, twelve men stood silently, awaiting instruction for their next missionary campaign. This group had just returned from a great feast—enough to feed five thousand men alone—from a handful of loaves and fishes broken and blessed by the hands of a carpenter's Son. They had witnessed a Canaanite woman's daughter get delivered from a vexing spirit, as one word was spoken by this Prophet. They had watched as this young Rabbi silenced the scoffing of the Sadducees and Pharisees.

Now they patiently waited to hear what their next assignment would be. But before another move was made, this strong Galilean stared deep within the souls of these men and asked, "Whom do men say that I am?"

Arresting their attention they began to utter the majority opinion and the talk on the streets by saying, "Some say you are John the Baptist." That was a great comparison! Only a few weeks earlier John himself sent forth word inquiring of this man, "Are you He spoken of by the prophets or shall we look for another?" Word was quickly returned, "Tell John the lame walk, the blind see and the deaf hear."

But still the disciples spoke, "Others say thou art Elias, Jeremias or one of the prophets." These were all insignificant by contrast, because turning and gazing at them with soul-piercing eyes, the Rabbi asked, "But whom do *you* say that I am?"

All stood speechless but one weathered fisherman, who nervously cleared his throat and, with every ounce of courage within him, exclaimed, "Thou art the Christ, the Anointed One, the Son of the living God!"

Pleased by the acclamation, Jesus assigned this fisherman a new name . . . the rock. Why? Because he received a divine revelation, birthed from the very heart of God, and it would be upon this proclamation that a mighty army, the church, would be built.

However, great revelation never comes without great tribulation. Simon Peter was now marked by God for blessing, and marked by Satan for destruction. This disclosure of the person of Jesus became the device which caused him to become the target of adulation and the target of adversity.

Satan sought to silence the knowledge once sealed in the hearts of mankind in the garden of Eden. In the same manner he had requisitioned Job, Satan stole away to the throne of God, striving to stop Peter as well.

With his scheming plot in place, Peter was not without his problems. Just a few months later, during the week of Passover, while gathered at the Last Supper, the Son of God shocked the disciples convened with Him with the words, "One among you will betray me."

Peter said in haste, "I will not, Lord!" But Jesus prophesied the path he would take and simply stated, "Before the cock crows three times you will betray me." Peter was a marked man.

Travel with me through the telescope of time and watch this same man stand before a crowd of thousands as he, along with John, preached the first evangelistic crusade of the infant church. This Peter, though tested and tried by trials and tribulation, was anointed on the Day of Pentecost by the Holy Spirit in a small upper room. Though he had been marked by Satan for destruction, he had also been marked by God for deliverance. He was a certain, or targeted, Christian.

In the hour you and I are living in, I believe there is a remnant church. I believe there is a people within a people and a man or woman within a family who are certain Christians and who have been targeted for the blessing of God.

However, maybe you feel lost in a whirlwind of the storms of life. Possibly you feel as though you are quickly sinking under the weight of insurmountable family problems. Perhaps sickness has struck your body and you feel as though you can't go on. If so, then this book is for you . . . the brokenhearted, beaten, bruised and oppressed. Look closely, because just over the horizon is an anchor of hope. You have been called and appointed by God in this year of Jubilee—the year of His favor.

3

The Spirit of the Lord has come upon you to anoint you with the fragrance which not only attracts the blessing of God, but also repels the attack of your adversary, the devil.

Read on . . . your mountain is just about ready to run into God's miracle. As you read through the pages of this book, I believe you will discover you are <u>marked</u> <u>for</u> <u>a</u> <u>miracle</u>!

Chapter 1

The Jubilee Anointing

On May 15, 1948 a royal blue and white flag, bearing as its insignia the star of David, was hoisted over a small piece of real estate in the center of the circumference of the earth. As that standard waved effortlessly in the Middle Eastern breeze, treaties were signed, handshakes were exchanged, and a nation was born . . . Israel. Painstakingly, through seemingly imminent annihilation, crisis and conflict, God's chosen people had reclaimed a homeland of their own.

For nearly 2,000 years Israel has not commemorated a spiritual Jubilee since its birth as a nation or since the destruction of its temple by Rome in 70 A.D. What exactly then is Jubilee? Leviticus 25:1-10 states:

> And the Lord spake unto Moses in mount Sinai, saying, Speak unto the children of Israel, and say unto them, When ye come into the land which I give you, then shall the land keep a sabbath unto the Lord. Six years thou shalt sow thy field, and six years thou shalt prune thy vineyard, and gather in the fruit thereof; but in the seventh year shall be a sabbath of rest unto the

land, a sabbath for the Lord: thou shalt neither sow thy field, nor prune thy vineyard.

That which groweth of its own accord of thy harvest thou shalt not reap, neither gather the grapes of thy vine undressed: for it is a year of rest unto the land. And the sabbath of the land shall be meat for you: for thee, and for thy servant, and for thy maid, and for thy hired servant, and for thy stranger that sojourneth with thee. And for thy cattle, and for the beast that are in thy land, shall all the increase thereof be meat.

And thou shalt number seven sabbaths of years unto thee, seven times seven years; and the space of the seven sabbaths of years shall be unto thee forty and nine years. Then shalt thou cause the trumpet of the jubilee to sound on the tenth day of the seventh month, in the day of atonement shall ye make the trumpet sound throughout all your land.

And ye shall hallow the fiftieth year, and proclaim liberty throughout all the land unto all the inhabitants thereof: it shall be a jubilee unto you; and ye shall return every man unto his possession, and ye shall return every man unto his family.

This fiftieth year sabbatical was a significant and momentous occasion for every Jewish person. Jubilee was a time of liberation, freedom and celebration. To the slave it meant release for him and his family from their taskmasters and to return to their own land. To every person it also signified a year when oppression from their adversaries ceased. To those held captive to debt, it was a year when all debts were canceled. Most importantly, the Year of Jubilee was a year when God Himself provided the harvest. It was a year when everything went back to God!

The Burden-Removing, Yoke-Destroying Anointing

There are literally hundreds of ways one could define the anointing of God. As a river travels across a terrain, trickling down rocks and crevices while leaving its mark by tracing out an intricate trail of its own, so is the anointing of God. When purposefully harnessed and released through your life, it can cool the fevered brow of an infant child. It can calm the cries of parents waiting for a call from a runaway teenager. It can still the tempest storms of trials and tribulations which Satan uses to assault your life.

Ezekiel described this potential power as waters steadily rising first around the ankles, then around the waist, until eventually its depth could not be measured for the magnitude of its manifestation. (Ezekiel 47.)

The prophet Hosea proclaimed that it was like rain coming down out of heaven. (Hosea 6:3.)

The Psalmist eloquently painted a panoramic picture of this yoke-destroying, burden-removing, tangible substance as a river which makes glad the city of God. (Psalm 46:4.)

John, the Beloved, illustrated it as an unction or special endowment from the Holy One. (1 John 2:20.)

The Bible's pages are lined with many accounts of how God's anointing was present in everything from a staff to a shadow. The anointing was resident in Moses' staff as it became a snake and swallowed the snakes of Pharaoh. It was resident in Elijah's mantel as he cast it upon the Jordan River, parting the waters so he could walk upon dry ground. The anointing was present upon Elisha's bones. When a dead man was cast into Elisha's open tomb, the dead man's eyes popped open and he lived again!

The anointing will cause that which was once dead to live again! It is the life force of Almighty God!

The anointing of God was in the mud Jesus placed upon the blind man's eyes; it was seen in Peter's shadow; it was present in Paul's handkerchiefs and aprons. And, I believe, that same anointing which invaded the borrowed tomb of Joseph of Arimathea and resurrected the three-day-old dead body of the Prince of Peace, Jesus Christ, is a tangible substance and can be transferred.

Isaiah 10:27 says of the anointing, "And it shall come to pass in that day, that his burden shall be taken away from off thy shoulder, and his yoke from off thy neck, and the yoke shall be destroyed because of the anointing."

There is a difference between break and destroy. When you break something it implies it can be put together again. When something is destroyed, however, it means to "cause it to cease to be as though it never existed."

For instance, take an expensive, beautiful vase, drop it and watch it break in two; however, it can be fixed again. Take that same vase, strike it with a hammer and shatter it into a million pieces. With glass lying like dust upon the floor, it is beyond any hope of being repaired. You are unable to tell a vase ever existed! That's what the anointing will do in your life! It will destroy the oppression of the adversary beyond restoration!

The yoke is any bondage which tries to oppress or take lordship, or authority, in any area of your life. If there is anything other than Jesus that has authority in your life, then there is a yoke upon you. But, the good news is, you can be delivered by the anointing that destroys every yoke!

My Uncle Willie is a perfect example of the yoke-destroying anointing. Willie was an alcoholic for 35 years and was never sober one day during that entire time. However, one day his family was able to get him to one of our church services. Even with a hangover from the night before, the Word of God was received by Willie in great power and demonstration.

Halfway through the message, the convicting power of the Holy Ghost came upon Willie, and he stood up, shook his finger and declared, "Enough is enough!"

The anointing of God ran through his body, and he has not had one drink in over 12 years! The anointing annihilated the yoke around his neck! When you allow the anointing of God to come into contact with your need, it will destroy every yoke and remove every burden!

The anointing is not an idea, a philosophy, a natural occurrence, or a thought. The anointing is a supernatural phenomenon! It has substance and power. It can be harnessed. It can be released, and it <u>will</u> <u>destroy</u> <u>every</u> <u>yoke</u>!

The Jubilee Anointing

When Jesus descended into the earth and wrapped Himself in flesh and blood, He was on an assignment of great importance. After successfully navigating through the temptation of the enemy for forty days in the wilderness, the Son of God proceeded to the synagogue. There the Bible records He broke the seals on the Torah and read from the prophet Isaiah:

> The Spirit of the Lord is upon me, because he hath anointed me to preach the gospel to the poor; he hath sent me to heal the brokenhearted, to preach deliverance to the captives, and recovering of sight to the blind, to set at liberty them that are bruised, to preach the acceptable year of the Lord.

> And he closed the book, and he gave it again to the minister, and sat down. And the eyes of all them that were in the synagogue were fastened on him. And he began to say unto them, This day is this scripture fulfilled in your ears (Luke 4:18-21).

History records that in every Jewish synagogue there was one very special seat. No one ever sat in it, however, because it was reserved for the coming Messiah. This was the reason the people, when Jesus closed the book and sat down in this reserved seat, became so mad that they grabbed Jesus by the nape of the neck to throw Him over the brow of the hill.

The announcement of the fulfillment of this Scripture both aroused and angered the religious rulers. They questioned among themselves, "Does He not realize this is not the time to celebrate Jubilee? Who does He think He is?"

Jesus knew exactly who He was . . . the Son of the Living God who had come to proclaim deliverance to the captives, recovering of sight to the blind and healing to all who would receive it.

What generations of people once waited to experience every fifty years was now being made available to them by Jesus. He was anointed first and foremost, to preach the good Gospel news to them!

The Hebrew word for anointing here translates, "to smear or to rub." The Amplified Bible in Luke 4:19 renders the acceptable year of the Lord as **the day when salvation and the free favors of God profusely abound**. I like to describe it this way: you are anointed, painted or marked with the fragrance which attracts the blessing and free favors of God!

Not only does Jehovah God want to target you for blessing, but also the devil has marked you for attack. He wants to steal what rightfully belongs to you. He is a thief. However, let me share with you an illustration.

In many banks there is a foolproof system for targeting a thief. For example, if a robber, with gun in hand, came into a bank and demanded all of the money, the teller would oblige the thief by complying with the order, filling a bag full of money and handing it to the thief. It may appear as if he escapes free from detection and apprehension, but what the thief doesn't realize is that the money he is carrying is marked!

Someone received the brilliant idea to make a dye pack which wraps around the money. When it is activated it releases a dye not only upon the money, but also upon the thief! Can you imagine the look upon his face when colored dye has exploded on him and his bag full of treasure? In the excitement and confusion, he may drop the money and still try to make a run for it. But the mark upon him will not come off. He will be found!

Proverbs 6:30-31 states, "Men do not despise a thief, if he steal to satisfy his soul when he is hungry; but if he be found, he shall restore sevenfold; he shall give all the substance of his house."

The word "found" in this verse means "to catch or apprehend." The devil may have stolen all of your possessions, your health and your family. He may be content in thinking he's taken everything from you. But just hold on, my child, joy is coming!

The anointing upon your life covers everything which belongs to you as well. Everything bearing your name is marked with an aroma which rises and attracts God's attention. He then dispatches His angels to apprehend your enemy. Satan will relinquish what belongs to you because he cannot stand to be surrounded by the anointed!

Take heart, because Satan has also been marked! Somewhere along the line he, too, will be uncovered and have to return sevenfold what he stole!

Second, Jesus was anointed to heal the brokenhearted. Hannah needed healing of a broken heart. (1 Samuel 1.) For years she had cried before the Lord because her womb was barren, and she could not have children. God heard her cry. When she was in such despair that she could no longer pray, the Lord of Hosts listened to her heart, and she conceived the prophet Samuel.

The ruler whose daughter had died was in need of healing from a broken heart. He had hope in this Canaan King, the carpenter's Son, so he went to Jesus and said,

"My daughter is even now dead: but come and lay thy hand upon her, and she shall live" (Matthew 9:18). The Bible goes on to say when Jesus entered his house that, "when the people were put forth, he went in, and took her by the hand, and the maid arose" (Matthew 9:25).

Jesus sees your deepest hurt, and it is His desire to touch the cold and callous place in your heart that you thought could never be healed. Even when Jesus was ridiculed for associating with publicans and sinners, in Matthew 9:12 He gave this response: "They that be whole need not a physician, but they that are sick."

The Psalmist declared, "He heals the heartbroken and bandages their wounds" (147:3 TMB).

Our Canaan King specializes in healing broken lives, broken dreams, broken homes, broken bodies and broken hearts. Not only will He heal your bruised, battered and broken heart, but He will also surgically remove the pain and torment of deep-seated wounds, for Psalm 51:17 in the Message Bible declares, "Heart-shattered lives ready for love don't for a moment escape God's notice."

Third, Jesus proclaimed deliverance to the captives. Recently, during the celebration of Jubilee in Israel, there was a movement in Parliament requesting the release of prisoners. This, in essence, is what happened every 50 years during Jubilee. Jesus came to declare that those held in bondage did not have to be captive to controlling desires, commanding addictions or anything that has taken hold in their life today.

Jesus did not wait until a specific time of day or week to heal or deliver a person. Specifically, according to Jewish tradition, it was not lawful to do this on the Sabbath, but this never deterred Him. He did not instruct them to come to the Sunday meeting or evangelistic crusade scheduled for some future time. Instead He released an anointing to each person He encountered wherever, whenever and in whatever condition He found them.

The Bible records that Christ healed a man with a withered hand on the Sabbath. (Mark 3.) He also touched a woman on the Sabbath who had an infirmity for 18 years. (Luke 13.). There is no need to wait for your deliverance because deliverance has been declared today!

Paul announced in 2 Corinthians 6:2, "Behold, now is the accepted time; behold, now is the day of salvation."

It does not matter to Jesus what religious holiday or day of the week it is! He still wants to see you set free! John 8:36 declares, "If the Son therefore shall make you free, ye shall be free indeed."

This is your day when despair and discouragement run headlong into the everlasting arms of God. Today—not tomorrow, next week, next month or next year—but today is your day of favor in every area of your life! You are **marked** for a miracle!

Lastly, the Jubilee Anointing upon Jesus, according to Luke 4, announced recovery of sight not only to the physically blind, but also to the spiritually blind.

In Acts 9 we have the story of Saul of Tarsus who ceaselessly persecuted the church of Jesus Christ. He was spiritually blind. But on the road to Damascus he was seized by the anointing of God, which struck him from his horse and temporarily blinded him. Jesus cried out, "Saul, Saul, why do you persecute me?" In a great display of repentance Saul cried out unto the Lord, was healed and became one of the greatest apostles, writing two-thirds of the New Testament.

Paul didn't seek after God, but God found him because He had need of him. He was marked by the Holy Ghost for a purpose.

Your loved ones may not be serving the Lord now, but rest assured, the scales of darkness are destined to fall off the eyes of those you have prayed for and believed to be saved. When the anointing comes into contact with those lost, without God, it will arrest their attention!

The Jubilee Anointing which rested upon Jesus is available to you now—to intercept every fiery dart of the wicked one. All that you must do is proclaim it in your life. He stands positioned to pour forth the tangible oil of His presence into your life!

Marked for Your Miracle

You and I are receptors of the Jubilee Anointing, so our every need will be met. In this final hour of human history, the Lord has come in a mighty display of His majesty. This is the year of the favor of the Lord, and you are **marked** for your miracle through the Jubilee Anointing! The significance of the Year of Jubilee cannot be adequately explained; it can only be experienced!

We are living in an hour when the last, greatest move of the Spirit of God is about to be unleashed throughout the earth. Joel 2:28,29 describes it this way:

> And it shall come to pass afterward, that I will pour out my spirit upon all flesh; and your sons and your daughters shall prophesy, your old men shall dream dreams, your young men shall see visions: and also upon the servants and upon the handmaids in those days will I pour out my spirit.

Etched upon the heart of every Christian is the emblem of a child of God. You and I have been chosen by

16

the Lord to bear His mark of sonship and to go forth in the unction of the Holy Spirit, to be partakers of all the blessings of Jubilee!

The Spirit of the Lord is upon you to enable you not only to live in the acceptable day of the favor of the Lord, but also to transcend above every onslaught of Satan. You have an anointing . . . a Jubilee Anointing to receive whatever you need from the Lord. If you need a healing, it is yours to claim. If you need deliverance, it too can be yours. Everything you need is available to you now! Today is your day of Jubilee!

Chapter 2

Painted Doorposts

The Israelites were gathered, each family in their own home, waiting for one last sign of the demonstration of God's divine power upon the head of Pharaoh. Moses had spoken irrevocable words to them just a few hours earlier:

Draw out and take you a lamb according to your families, and kill the passover.

And ye shall take a bunch of hyssop, and dip it in the blood that is in the bason, and strike the lintel and the two side posts with the blood that is in the bason; and none of you shall go out at the door of his house until the morning.

For the Lord will pass through to smite the Egyptians; and when he seeth the blood upon the lintel, and on the two side posts, the Lord will pass over the door, and will not suffer the destroyer to come in unto your houses to smite you (Exodus 12:21-23).

The Lord was positioned for one final blow to Pharaoh's dynasty. He was prepared once and for all to display his power among the Egyptians. This would be His last demonstration against the alien forces who had enslaved His chosen people.

Satan made one final effort to stop the liberation of Israel. However, the last bastion of satanic resistance always comes right before your breakthrough.

For instance, just before the children of Israel were preparing to leave Egyptian bondage, Pharaoh made one last attempt to seal their fate forever as slaves. He had attempted before to play "let's make a deal" with them, as to compel them to worship their God in the land of bondage. Moses' response was, "We will go three days' journey into the wilderness, and sacrifice to the Lord our God, as he shall command us" (Exodus 8:27).

The Bible bears out that Pharaoh's heart was hardened all the more.

Then he said, "Leave your cattle," because he knew they couldn't live without a source of supply.

Then he ordered them to leave their children. But on this day, the climax of this standoff was about to occur. Jehovah of Hosts, the Lord God Himself, made the proclamation to go throughout the land and take branches of hyssop soaked in blood and then strike them upon the lintel of every Jewish home.

Let me **paint** for you another picture. Hyssop, a very aromatic plant, was taken and dipped in blood. The blood, or the anointing, was then "painted," if you will, upon every door. I want to stop and remind you that you are painted with the fragrance which attracts the blessing and favor of

God! What was the result? The children of Israel were protected and spared from death!

The anointing has everything to do with Jesus' covenant with the Heavenly Father and nothing to do with you. You cannot earn His anointing and blessing. You cannot obtain your answer by good works.

For instance, if you look through the pages of your Bible, you will discover that it was God who found Abraham in Ur of the Chaldees. It was the Lord who sought Jacob at Bethel and marked him with an anointing. It was Jesus who pursued Paul on the road to Damascus.

In fact The Message Bible plainly states in Psalm chapter 16 verse 5: "My choice is you, God, first and only. And now I find I'm your choice! You set me up with a house and yard. And then you made me your heir!" You are God's favorite!

Authority and Anointing

The importance of being painted goes beyond the lintels of the doorposts of the Israelites. They had something which allowed them to stand in the anointing of the Lord, and that was the authority of His Word.

Jesus, Himself, possessed an authority as well, for our key Scripture in Luke 4:14 says, "And Jesus returned in the power of the Spirit into Galilee: and there went out a fame of him through all the region round about."

The fame of Jesus began to spread. Why? Because of the many signs and wonders He performed. You are destined to see signs and wonders. You are to bear witness of the mighty acts of God. You are supposed to be a signpost, pointing people to Jesus. People care more about your walk than they do about your talk. They want to hear the reports of cancer disappearing and of deliverance taking place!

This is how the fame of this revival is going to spread. It's not going to spread by how many handbills we buy. It is going to spread when the people of God begin to be signposts directing others to God. The Gospel of Luke goes on to say:

> And he taught in their synagogues, being glorified of all. And he came to Nazareth, where he had been brought up: and, as his custom was, he went into the synagogue on the sabbath day, and stood up for to read.
>
> And there was delivered unto him the book of the prophet Esaias. And when he had opened the book, he found the place where it was written,
>
> The Spirit of the Lord is upon me, because he hath anointed me to preach the gospel to the poor; he hath sent me to heal the brokenhearted, to preach deliverance to the captives, and recovering of sight to the blind, to set at liberty them that are bruised,
>
> To preach the acceptable year of the Lord. And he closed the book, and he gave it again to the minister,

and sat down. And the eyes of all them that were in the synagogue were fastened on him (Luke 4:15-20).

Those gathered in the synagogue began to exclaim among themselves, "Who does He think He is? I think it is very evident who He thought He was. I think it's very evident who God thought He was. I think it's very evident that we should let people know who He is. He is the Son of God.

But ask yourself this question. How much of a higher anointing can you get than God? Why did God have to anoint Jesus? Because Philippians 2:5-11 says:

Let this mind be in you, which was also in Christ Jesus: Who, being in the form of God, thought it not robbery to be equal with God:

But made himself of no reputation, and took upon him the form of a servant, and was made in the likeness of men: and being found in fashion as a man, he humbled himself, and became obedient unto death, even the death of the cross.

Wherefore God also hath highly exalted him, and given him a name which is above every name: that at the name of Jesus every knee should bow, of things in heaven, and things in earth, and things under the earth; and that every tongue should confess that Jesus Christ is Lord, to the glory of God the Father.

Acts 10:38 states of Jesus, "How God anointed Jesus of Nazareth with the Holy Ghost and with power: who went about doing good, and healing all that were oppressed of the devil; for God was with him."

Have you ever noticed that some people act kind of strange around people that have an anointing . . . especially around their own hometown? It was hard for people to believe Jesus was anointed.

Many only had a partial revelation of Jesus Christ, the Anointed One. Some saw Him only as a carpenter. Others believed Him to be just a prophet. Still the popular opinion among some was that He was a king. Why, even those who saw Jesus walk upon the water perceived Him to be a ghost. But Jesus was anointed by the Holy Spirit of God!

However, Jesus didn't go around calling Himself the Son of God. He called Himself the Son of Man. What was one of the ways He exercised His authority? Hebrews 6:1,2 says:

Therefore leaving the principles of the doctrine of Christ, let us go on unto perfection; not laying again the foundation of repentance from dead works, and of faith toward God, of the doctrine of baptisms, and of laying on of hands, and of resurrection of the dead, and of eternal judgment.

These are the foundational doctrines of the Christian faith. The laying on of hands is one of the major doctrines of our faith. If you are hooked up with a church that does not practice these doctrines, you are not hooked up with a New Testament church. You may be hooked up with a religious organization, but if they are not obeying the basic doctrines and tenets of the Christian faith, then they are not a New Testament church.

There is a reason and a purpose for the laying on of hands. Something happens when hands are laid upon you. That is the reason the Bible says to lay hands on no man suddenly, because during the laying on of hands there is a transference of the anointing of God. It is a tangible thing, and I want to make this profound statement: it is housed within your body.

The anointing is not floating around out there somewhere. Jesus didn't say the anointing is hanging around. Jesus didn't say the anointing is a kind of pseudo-spiritual cosmic thought. He said the Spirit of the Lord is upon Me. It's on me. It's in me. It's through me. It's tangible on my body!

John 5:26,27 states, "For as the Father hath life in himself, so hath He given to the Son to have life in Himself. And hath given Him authority to execute judgment also because He is the Son of man."

Most people do not have a problem realizing we are the sons of men. One translation says He hath given Him authority for and against to execute judgment. He hath given Him authority for us and against the devil to execute judgment. God's going to judge for you and against the devil.

Authority in the earth realm comes to you because you have an earth suit. In other words, you have authority on this earth because you have a body. You could not accomplish anything without a body!

The Bible also says, God is a Spirit, and they that worship Him must worship Him in Spirit and in truth. Herein lies one of the answers to one of the greatest questions that plagues the minds of men.

If God is a loving God, why are people starving to death? Why are wars and rumors of wars all over the face of the earth? Why is there drug addiction? Why is there cocaine addiction? Why are hospital beds full?

Let me point out something to you. Genesis 1:26, 27 states, "And God said, Let us make man in our image, after our likeness: and let them have dominion over the fish of the sea, and over the fowl of the air, and over the cattle, and over all the earth, and over every creeping thing that creepeth upon the earth. So God created man in his own image, in the image of God created he him; male and female created he them."

Now go with me to a point in time when Jesus said, "Verily, verily, I say unto you, He that entereth not by the door into the sheepfold, but climbeth up some other way, the same is a thief and a robber. But he that entereth in by the door is the shepherd of the sheep" (John 10:1,2).

What is He referring to? He is referring to the devil. The devil gained entry into this earth illegally! He is a reprobate, an intruder, and he has come here illegally! The reason is that he has no body!

But I want to make a very important point. Due to the way God set up authority, He, Himself, being a Spirit, cannot do anything without a body. That's the reason He said, The eyes of the Lord run to and fro throughout the whole earth that He might show Himself strong on behalf of all those whose hearts are perfected for Him.

That's the reason He said be _filled_ with the Spirit. Why didn't He say for the Spirit to get filled with you? He's talking about the Spirit getting inside you. Why? Because a spirit being without a body has no authority in this earth; therefore, neither does Satan! He is a thief and a robber. You have authority in the earth, and you have a body to prove it!

I like the way this great praise song says it:

Jesus has all authority here! For this habitation was fashioned for the Lord's presence! Jesus has all authority here!

However, consider this: If Jesus did the mighty signs, wonders and miracles He did because He was the Son of God, why didn't He do any of them until he was 30 years old? The Bible bears out the entire ministry of Jesus transpired from the time He was baptized by John in the River Jordan. Coming up straightway out of the water there appeared a dove and lighted upon Him, symbolizing the Holy Ghost baptism. A voice spoke out of heaven, "This is my beloved Son. In Him I am well pleased."

The authority of having an earth suit gives you the *opportunity* to manifest miracles, but the anointing gives you the *ability* to manifest miracles.

Immediately following the proclamation that He was the Messiah and the anointing was upon His life, Jesus entered into Peter's house and ministered to his mother-in-law. Luke 4:40,41 proclaims:

> Now when the sun was setting, all they that had any sick with divers diseases brought them unto him; and he laid his hands on every one of them, and healed them.

> And devils also came out of many, crying out, and saying, Thou art Christ the Son of God. And he rebuking them suffered them not to speak: for they knew that he was Christ.

One thing you must realize about devils is that they are liars. Satan is the father of all lies. He never tells the truth unless telling the truth is to his advantage.

The demon hordes of hell were actually saying, "You can't torment us. You are the Son of God. You have no authority on the earth. We know you. You are God, and you don't have any authority in the earth realm."

But Jesus' response was, "Shut up and come out of them!"

These demons were challenging Jesus' authority. They were saying He was the Son of God. You can't do this. In Matthew 8:29, these same demons said, "Don't torment us, thou Son of God. It is not the time. You can't torment us before the time."

He couldn't have tormented them if He was just the Son of God, but He wasn't just the Son of God. He wasn't just Spirit. He was born of a virgin; He came through the door (John 10:1). He had authority as a man on the face of this earth!

The same Jubilee Anointing which empowered Jesus has been given to you. You have authority in every area of your life!

Maybe you feel trapped in an endless cycle of the onslaught of Satan and you say, "I don't feel anointed! I feel as though I'm the one who is being railroaded by the devil. But 1 John 3:2 says, "Beloved, it doth not yet appear what we shall be: but we know that when he shall appear, we shall be like him; for we shall see him as he is." Isn't that what it said? Beloved, now are we the sons of God. And it doth not yet appear what we shall be, but we are going to be something better than we are now! You have authority and anointing in the earth!

A Target for Breakthrough

During the Gulf War, when a fighter pilot had locked onto his target, the code word was that the target was **painted.** You may be facing one of life's darkest trials, tests or tragedies, but that is no obstacle in the eyes of your God. He will seek you out and **mark** you for your miracle!

29

Don't allow the devil to undermine your miracle! You are **marked** with the fragrance which attracts the favor and blessing of the Lord! You are painted or, rather, you are a target!

Jesus has come to paint the doorpost of your heart with His anointing. He has come to put His **mark** upon you as His child. Our Canaan King has descended to paint your home with His **anointed** presence.

What then can Satan do to you? How can he affect your life or your family? When the alien armies of the Antichrist assail themselves against you in full battle array and they see the blood painted upon your life and your loved ones they will have to pass over!

You may say, I need a job; or I need a healing in my body; I need to be free from addiction; I need renewal in my spirit. Job 22:28 proclaims, "You shall also decide and decree a thing, and it shall be established for you; and the light [of God's favor] shall shine upon your ways."

You may say, "But my family is not living for God!" The Book of Job goes on to say in verse 30 that God, "Will even deliver the one [for whom you intercede] who is not innocent; yes, he will be delivered through the cleanness of YOUR hands."

God is in the healing and delivering business. This is the year of liberation, and by His anointing He wants to deliver you from sin, sickness, disease, depression and every devastating blow of the enemy!

Through this Jubilee Anointing, it is the deep desire of the Lord to touch every area of your life with the oil of

His Spirit. He wants to restore families and marriages everywhere. God wants to paint those in pain with His healing anointing. God wants to paint the doorpost of those broken in heart with a healing balm.

The Holy Ghost's radar is locked in on you right now. You may not know how you will survive the insurmountable mountain facing your life, but God has already planned your escape and anointed you to receive your breakthrough! You are anointed!

Chapter 3

A Residue of Hope

Battered and beaten, the Israelites fearfully fought their foes, the Moabites. The reason for their conflict was because of sin and idolatry. Though tirelessly they contended against their enemy, their defeat was sealed by the prophetic words uttered by an annoying standard bearer of righteousness and holiness, who refused to allow their nation to be a casualty of compromise. However, he fell to the sting of death and his prophetic voice was forever silenced.

Fatalities of the conflict were catastrophic and all too common. Young and old alike were among the slain, and there was barely enough time to even bury the dead.

One young Jewish boy among the ranks, in particular, stood out on this dreadful day. Though this was his first battle, he did not lack bravery or fortitude. Fearlessly he took his position on the front line, face to face with Israel's archenemy. And fearlessly, as he was struck by a stray arrow, he gave his life for his country.

During a small break in the callous war, and not willing to leave his body as so many others — carnage upon the country's landscape — a special ceremony was held in his honor. As his body was being made ready for burial, upon the horizon appeared a battalion of soldiers. In haste to position themselves again for another assault, the few Israelite warriors tossed his lifeless frame into an open sepulcher where another lay . . . an anointed prophet.

There the young lad lay, and there he would stay until his bones were bleached in the desert sun . . . or would he?

As if invaded by an unseen force, his hollow shell began to move . . . first a finger, then an eyelid. His frame became empowered with an energy greater than death itself, and life was breathed back into his body.

What was it that apprehended the body of this young soldier? It was the anointing . . . the Jubilee Anointing. The bones of Elisha, the prophet, lay in this tomb, and though his spirit had departed into the bosom of Abraham, the mantel of the anointing of the Lord still rested upon him.

The Tangible Anointing

As in the story of the resurrected young soldier, we see that the anointing of God is tangible. The mantel which rested upon Elisha, though he was absent from his body, clung to his bones like a blanket. Throughout his life and the life of his mentor Elijah, the tangible Jubilee Anointing was prevalent.

The anointing which was upon Elijah, for instance, caused him to be able to outrun Ahab's chariots when he prophesied "an abundance of rain." In 1 Kings 17:17-22, we also see a display of God's mighty power:

And it came to pass after these things, that the son of the woman, the mistress of the house, fell sick; and his sickness was so sore, that there was no breath left in him. And she said unto Elijah, What have I to do with thee, O thou man of God? art thou come unto me to call my sin to remembrance, and to slay my son?

And he said unto her, Give me thy son. And he took him out of her bosom, and carried him up into a loft, where he abode, and laid him upon his own bed. And he cried unto the Lord, and said, O Lord my God, hast thou also brought evil upon the widow with whom I sojourn, by slaying her son?

And he stretched himself upon the child three times, and cried unto the Lord, and said, O Lord my God, I pray thee, let this child's soul come into him again. And the Lord heard the voice of Elijah; and the soul of the child came into him again, and he revived.

This widow and her son had been sustained through famine by the word of the man of God. When the water around them became nothing more than dust, and when everything was dying, the Word of God bears out that their oil and meal did not fail.

But somewhere along the line, her son fell ill while Elijah was staying with them. Oh, how often it seems as though the anointing of God is touching everyone else's life, healing everyone else, and delivering everyone else,

35

while our own dream is dying. Just like an incurable cancer, there was no hope and no cure for the disease of death!

This woman accused the man of God for coming to her house, sustaining them through famine, only to allow her son to die! But may I remind you that the Jubilee Anointing will cause that which was once dead to live again! Your dead dreams will live again!

Elijah did not attempt to make excuses for her predicament. Instead, he replied, "Bring the boy to me!" And, when the widow did, Elijah stretched himself upon the child and he was resurrected from the dead!

You may feel as though Jesus is in the house and everyone around you is singing and praising the Lord. Tears are rolling down the cheeks of the saints of God, with hands uplifted, as they worship at the throne of the Master. And Jesus says to you, "Bring your broken dreams to me. Bring the pain of your past and your broken heart to me."

Jesus came to proclaim your Jubilee today. You are marked for a miracle. All you must do is take one step toward him, and He will run to you.

Jesus will go to any length to get you your miracle. Why? Because there is a Jubilee Anointing to proclaim liberty to the captives, recovering of sight to the blind and deliverance to all who are oppressed! He has targeted you for blessing.

Painted with Hope

Jeremiah 29:11 says, "For I know the thoughts and plans that I have for you, says the Lord, thoughts and plans for welfare and peace and not for evil, to give you hope in your final outcome" (AMP).

There is a hope in Jesus. When you are painted with the anointing of the Lord, you are infused with hope for your final outcome. Regardless of the situation or what the circumstances surrounding your life look like, you have steadfast confidence and assurance that everything is going to be all right.

What is hope? It is favorable and confident expectation to do with the "unseen" and "future" happy anticipation of good. Hebrews 11:1 says, "Now faith is the substance of things hoped for, the evidence of things not seen."

Let me share with you a story of hope from 2 Kings 4. Elisha (who performed twice the miracles of his predecessor, Elijah, because of the double portion of the anointing which was upon him) was passing through Shunem. While there a Shunammite woman treated him with the honor due him as a prophet of God. She and her husband gave him food, and even went so far as to build him a room so that every time he passed through town, he would have a place to stay.

One day while Elisha stopped there to rest, he called for this woman. Because of all the kindness she had shown to Elisha, he requested of her, "What can I do for you?"

Let me interject here that Matthew 10:41 says, "He that receiveth a prophet in the name of a prophet shall receive a prophet's reward; and he that receiveth a righteous man in the name of a righteous man shall receive a righteous man's reward."

This woman could have asked for anything. She could have requested an audience with the king. She could have requested a great influx of wealth. However, her only desire was to conceive a child. The desire of her heart was granted, and she bore a son.

Verses 18-28 and 32-35 of 2 Kings 4 go on to reveal:

And when the child was grown, it fell on a day, that he went out to his father to the reapers. And he said unto his father, My head, my head. And he said to a lad, Carry him to his mother.

And when he had taken him, and brought him to his mother, he sat on her knees till noon, and then died. And she went up, and laid him on the bed of the man of God, and shut the door upon him, and went out.

And she called unto her husband, and said, Send me, I pray thee, one of the young men, and one of the asses, that I may run to the man of God, and come again. And he said, Wherefore wilt thou go to him to day? it is neither new moon, nor sabbath. And she said, It shall be well. Then she saddled an ass, and said to her servant, Drive, and go forward; slack not thy riding for me, except I bid thee.

So she went and came unto the man of God to mount Carmel. And it came to pass, when the man of God saw her afar off, that he said to Gehazi his servant, Behold, yonder is that Shunammite: Run now, I pray thee, to meet her, and say unto her, Is it well with thee? is it well with thy husband? is it well with the child? And she answered, It is well.

And when she came to the man of God to the hill, she caught him by the feet: but Gehazi came near to thrust her away. And the man of God said, Let her alone; for her soul is vexed within her: and the Lord hath hid it from me, and hath not told me. Then she said, Did I desire a son of my lord? did I not say, Do not deceive me?

And when Elisha was come into the house, behold, the child was dead, and laid upon his bed. He went in therefore, and shut the door upon them twain, and prayed unto the Lord.

And he went up, and lay upon the child, and put his mouth upon his mouth, and his eyes upon his eyes, and his hands upon his hands: and he stretched himself upon the child; and the flesh of the child waxed warm. Then he returned, and walked in the house to and fro; and went up, and stretched himself upon him: and the child sneezed seven times, and the child opened his eyes.

This woman could have given up on her dream of raising a child. She could have resigned herself to the fact that her son was dead and believed there was nothing she could do about it. However, faith never fears fact. Faith does not give up due to F-E-A-R (False Evidence which Appears Real). The cry of her heart was, "It is well!" When Elijah burst forth on the scene, the anointing flooded the body of this young boy and he came to life again!

As I pointed out in Jeremiah 29, the Jubilee Anointing comes to give you hope in your final outcome! The anointing of God will make you see things differently than anyone else sees them.

When the doctors look at you and say you have to die and cannot live, faith will answer the door and drive out fear. When mourning for a lost loved one surpasses the hope for a better day, God will give you the garment of praise. You can stand in the face of the adversary and say, "It is well!"

The Oil of Joy for Mourning

In the Year of Jubilee, the Lord wants to mark you with an anointing which will propel you through every line of Satan's defense. As you have read in previous chapters, it is from Luke 4 that Jesus proclaims the Jubilee

Anointing, but it is from the Book of Isaiah that He is actually reading.

One verse in particular, which He did not quote is, "To grant [consolation and joy] to those who mourn in Zion—to give them an ornament (a garland or diadem) of beauty instead of ashes, the oil of joy instead of mourning, the garment [expressive] of praise instead of a heavy, burdened, and failing spirit—that they may be called oaks of righteousness [lofty, strong, and magnificent, distinguished for uprightness, justice, and right standing with God], the planting of the Lord, that He may be glorified (Isaiah 61:3 AMP).

The Lord wants to give you the oil of joy for mourning. He wants to anoint you with an anointing which will transcend every circumstance you may face. The Shunammite woman was anointed with the oil of joy, because the only words she could say when facing death itself were, "It is well!"

The Psalmist said of this oil, "Thou lovest righteousness, and hatest wickedness: therefore God, thy God, hath anointed thee with the oil of gladness above thy fellows" (Psalm 45:7).

What is the oil of joy? The actual translation is a shining forth of cheerful anticipation for mourning. In Isaiah 61, the Lord said He would give unto you the garment of praise for the spirit of heaviness. What is the garment of praise? It is a cover of celebration for the spirit of hopelessness. Hopelessness implies acceptance or resignation to the current situation with no future anticipation of change.

The enemy is engaged in an all-out onslaught to stop you and cause hopelessness to invade your heart. The Bible says, "Be sober, be vigilant; because your adversary the devil, as a roaring lion, walketh about, seeking whom he may devour" (1 Peter 5:8).

But when he comes along to distract or destroy you, Jesus promised, "And I will pray the Father, and he shall give you another Comforter, that he may abide with you for ever" (John 14:16). God will replace your hopeless heart with a Jubilee Anointing of celebration!

Mephibosheth, Jonathan's son and Saul's grandson, is a perfect example of someone who could have settled for his current condition. He was camped out in a place called Machir, which is better known as "sold out." He was content with hopelessness. But King David found him and took him to his house, gave him his inheritance and treated him as one of his sons.

Jesus will do the same for you. He will take you out of the house of mourning and put you in the house of feasting, and cover you with praise and His favor. The Lord will paint you with a Jubilee Anointing and give you a hope to sustain you through every attack of the enemy!

Chapter 4

The Acceptable Time

Nearly 2,000 years ago, our Canaan King, before the Spirit of the Lord anointed Him with power and majesty, fasted for 40 days in the wilderness. He was tempted, tested and tried, and successfully subdued the prince of the power of the air, Satan himself, with the penetrating statement, "It is written!"

Full of the Holy Spirit, this strong Galilean then proceeded to Nazareth. As was His custom, the Bible says He entered the synagogue on the Sabbath day. The magnitude of the moment was signified by the silence among the masses, as the Savior stood up to read. Our Canaan King boldly proclaimed:

> The Spirit of the Lord is upon me, because he has anointed me to preach the gospel to the poor; he hath sent me to heal the brokenhearted, to preach deliverance to the captives, and recovering of sight to the blind, to set at liberty them that are bruised, to preach the acceptable year of the Lord (Luke 4:18,19).

Jesus became our Jubilee—our Great Liberator! And, though Jubilee was still several months away, our Reigning

King had announced its arrival. Though it was not depicted by a day on the calendar, Jesus declared, "This is the acceptable day or the day when My *free favors* profusely abound!" In this Year of Jubilee, God has already made the provision for us to possess our promised land!

Flies in the Ointment
Satan is scheming to distract you from walking in the Jubilee Anointing and being marked for your miracle. But God provided a solution to silence him. Joel chapter 2 says,

> Blow ye the trumpet in Zion, and sound an alarm in my holy mountain: let all the inhabitants of the land tremble: for the day of the Lord cometh, for it is nigh at hand;
>
> Therefore also now, saith the Lord, turn ye even to me with all your heart, and with fasting, and with weeping, and with mourning: And rend your heart, and not your garments, and turn unto the Lord your God: for he is gracious and merciful, slow to anger, and of great kindness, and repenteth him of the evil.
>
> Who knoweth if he will return and repent, and leave a blessing behind him; even a meat offering and a drink offering unto the Lord your God? Blow the trumpet in Zion, sanctify a fast, call a solemn assembly:

Gather the people, sanctify the congregation, assemble the elders, gather the children, and those that suck the breasts: let the bridegroom go forth of his chamber, and the bride out of her closet.

Let the priests, the ministers of the Lord, weep between the porch and the altar, and let them say, Spare thy people, O Lord, and give not thine heritage to reproach, that the heathen should rule over them: wherefore should they say among the people, Where is their God?

Be glad then, ye children of Zion, and rejoice in the Lord your God: for he hath given you the former rain moderately, and he will cause to come down for you the rain, the former rain, and the latter rain in the first month.

And the floors shall be full of wheat, and the fats shall overflow with wine and oil. And I will restore to you the years that the locust hath eaten, the cankerworm, and the caterpillar, and the palmerworm, my great army which I sent among you (vv. 1, 12-17, 23-26).

God commanded the children of Israel to call a solemn assembly and to fast. Why? In order to repent so He could turn away their captivity and pour out His blessing upon them.

E.M. Bounds once said, "Water cannot rise above its own level." A spotless prayer cannot flow from a spotted heart.

Over the year, I've studied the lives of people such as Smith Wigglesworth and Dr. Lester Sumrall, and I've often wondered how they were able to walk in such a consistent level of faith and anointing. I discovered that not only did they fast, but they also lived a fasted lifestyle.

There was a group of people in Numbers 6 who did this, as well. They were called Nazarites, and they took a vow that they would drink no strong drink and they would not cut their hair. Why? Because they made the choice to be sanctified unto the Lord.

These were they who were part of a remnant. God is looking for a people who live separated lives today. He is looking for those who refuse to become a part of the religious order of their day. They are those who live a fasted life because they hunger for something more!

Not long ago, I was in a gun store and saw a nickel plated, double barreled gun with dogs engraved on the side that looked just like mine. I had the money to buy it, but I decided against it. Why? Because I wanted it, and I wanted to discipline myself to say, "No." I want to live a fasted lifestyle before God.

Fasting will give you power over the adversary. A wonderful example of this message was taught to the disciples by Jesus in Matthew 17. A father brought his son to Him and said,

Lord, have mercy on my son: for he is lunatick, and sore vexed: for ofttimes he falleth into the fire, and oft into the water. And I brought him to thy disciples, and they could not cure him.

Then Jesus answered and said, O faithless and perverse generation, how long shall I be with you? how long shall I suffer you? bring him hither to me. And Jesus rebuked the devil; and he departed out of him: and the child was cured from that very hour.

Then came the disciples to Jesus apart, and said, Why could not we cast him out? And Jesus said unto them, Because of your unbelief: for verily I say unto you, If ye have faith as a grain of mustard seed, ye shall say unto this mountain, Remove hence to yonder place; and it shall remove; and nothing shall be impossible unto you. Howbeit this kind goeth not out but by *prayer and fasting* (vv. 15-21).

The disciples could not cast the spirit out of the lunatic boy because of unbelief. But Jesus went on to say, "This kind cometh not out but by prayer and fasting."

You can fast without praying and it has an effect. You can pray without fasting and it has an effect. But when you combine praying and fasting, you then target your need with the greatest spiritual strength available to you.

Faith needs prayer for growth and development, but prayer needs fasting for growth and development. Fasting means to abstain from something, and it does not necessarily have to be food. Adam and Eve were commanded to fast from the tree of knowledge of good and evil.

The reason so many in the body of Christ are not the spiritual giants they want to be is because they give their body everything it wants! Instead, we fast the wrong man. We fast our spirit man, only allowing it to eat during Sunday and midweek church services, while we feed our body three meals a day plus dessert.

Here is another spiritual lesson: the more God blesses you, the more you need to check your flesh. The quickest way to access the spirit world is to deny your flesh. Romans 8:13 declares to us to "mortify the deeds of the body."

2 Timothy 3:2-5 states:

As the end approaches, people are going to be self-absorbed, money-hungry, self-promoting, stuck-up, profane, contemptuous of parents, crude, coarse, dog-eat-dog, unbending, slanderers, impulsively wild, savage, cynical, treacherous, ruthless, bloated, windbags, addicted to lust and allergic to God. They'll make a show of religion, but behind the scenes they're animals" (TMB).

Many cults use fasting because they believe it aids them with the cooperation of demon spirits. Why? Because it puts down their flesh and elevates the spirit realm. When I was in Singapore, I viewed men who had fasted for 30 days from sunrise to sunset.

After this time they would take large needles, thicker than a coat hanger, and they would pull their tongues out and pierce through their top lips, through their tongue and through their bottom lips, so that their tongues were protruding out. I watched them take hundreds of similar needles and pierce their bodies. During all of this, not one drop of blood spilled from their bodies.

They would then tie carts, loaded with children, to those needles piercing their bodies. Then they would pull them through the streets in 110 degree weather without breaking a sweat. Why? They were in a spiritual trance. They had received the aid of demon spirits, because they had denied their flesh and opened up their spirits to demon spirits.

If the devil's kingdom can have those kinds of results, what do you think will happen when we learn to put our flesh under subjection and open up our lives to the Holy Ghost?

Let me share with you another example. So many know the story of the destruction of Sodom and Gomorrah and the tragic events surrounding Lot's escape. But I believe few really understand the sin which caused their downfall. Ezekiel 16:49 states,

Behold, this was the iniquity of thy sister Sodom, pride, fulness of bread, and abundance of idleness was in her and in her daughters, neither did she strengthen the hand of the poor and needy.

Sodom fell because they were arrogant and lived in careless ease, and because they were overrun with an abundance of food. Unfortunately, this is the state so many in America and other countries suffer from.

In Paul's discourse to the Corinthians he said,

Just because something is technically legal doesn't mean that it's spiritually appropriate. If I went around doing whatever I thought I could get by with, I'd be a slave to my whims. You know the old saying, "First you eat to live, then you live to eat"?

Well it may be true that the body is only a temporary thing, but that's no excuse for stuffing your body with food or indulging it with sex. Since the Master honors you with a body, you ought to honor Him with your body (I Corinthians 6:12,13 TMB).

Isaiah 58:1, 3-7 shows another important parallel with the Jubilee Anointing:

Cry loud, spare not, lift up thy voice like a trumpet and shew my people their transgression, and the house of Jacob their sins.

Wherefore have we fasted, say they, and thou seest not? wherefore have we afflicted our soul, and thou takest no knowledge? Behold, in the day of your fast ye find pleasure, and exact all your labours.

Behold, ye fast for strife and debate, and to smite with the fist of wickedness: ye shall not fast as you do this day, to make your voice be heard on high. Is it such a fast that I have chosen? a day for a man to afflict his soul? is it to bow down his head as a bulrush, and to spread sackcloth and ashes under him? wilt thou call this a fast, and an acceptable day of the Lord?

Is not this the fast that I have chosen? to loose the bands of wickedness, to undo the heavy burdens, and to let the oppressed go free, and to break every yoke? Is it not to deal thy bread to the hungry, and that thou bring the poor that are cast out to thy house? when thou seest the naked, that thou cover him; and that thou hide not thyself from thine own flesh?

Let me paraphrase for you what I believe the Lord was saying. He said, "I want you to become so spiritually strong that because you have denied your flesh, not only have you loosed the bands of wickedness in your own life, but also you're able to proclaim the acceptable year and day of the Lord by dealing your bread to the hungry."

The Lord was not just talking about natural bread. He was referring to taking that which has sustained you and giving it to someone else.

When you fast and go in the strength of the anointing which is upon you, then you can loose the bands of wickedness. You can let the oppressed go free, and undo the heavy burdens and break every yoke!

Many people fast for different periods of time. Our church recently was called to fast 40 days. Why? When you pray and fast consistently for 40 days at the same time about the same situation something supernatural begins to happen.

Jesus fasted 40 days and was tempted of the devil before He made his appearance in the synagogue and announced, "The Spirit of the Lord is upon me."

Jesus was seen for 40 days after His resurrection, speaking of the things that pertained to the Kingdom of God. And, He was proved to be alive after His passion by many infallible proofs.

Women are pregnant for 9 months, which equates to 40 weeks, before giving birth. I believe in 40 days you can give birth to the most awesome spiritual miracle you could ever dream possible. You'll give birth to it if you let it grow in there for 40 days. But when you're pregnant, you have to be careful what you eat and drink.

Ecclesiastes 10:1 says, "Dead flies cause the ointment of the apothecary to send forth a stinking savour: so doth a little folly him that is in reputation for wisdom and honour."

The word ointment here is translated "anointing." When the anointing is penetrated by flies, it causes it to grow stale and useless. Satan is better known as Beelzebub, or the "Father of Flies," or of tormenting spirits.

Jesus was criticized by the religious rulers who said,

This fellow doth not cast out devils, but by Beelzebub the prince of the devils. And Jesus knew their thoughts, and said unto them, Every kingdom divided against itself is brought to desolation; and every city or house divided against itself shall not stand:

And if Satan cast out Satan, he is divided against himself; how shall then his kingdom stand? And if I by Beelzebub cast out devils, by whom do your children cast them out? therefore they shall be your judges. But if I cast out devils by the Spirit of God, then the kingdom of God is come unto you (Matthew 12:24-28).

The kingdom of God has come nigh you today. Fasting is a powerful tool against the adversary and will allow you to gain authority in every area of your life. When you begin to fast, I believe the spirit of infirmity, lack, bondage and anything tormenting your life will die. The flies of demonic power will not only be broken off of your life, but also they will be destroyed because of the anointing! (Isaiah 10:27).

Tradition: The Thief of Power

Tradition is another adversary which will stop the flow of God's anointing in your life. In Mark 7 the Pharisees were questioning Jesus and his disciples for not walking after the custom, or "tradition," of the elders.

But Jesus' response to them was, "This people honoureth me with their lips but their heart is far from me" (vs. 6). He accused them of rejecting the commandments of God in order to fulfill their own man-made traditions. The result, as stated in verse 13, was that they made, "the word of God of none effect through your tradition, which ye have delivered: and many such like things do ye."

One of our church elders shares a brilliant story which vividly portrays what tradition will do to you. A young woman, who had not been married very long, began to prepare supper for her husband. She prepared a nice ham, but before she put it in the oven to bake, she cut off both ends . . . something she had watched her mother do.

One day as she was again preparing dinner and another ham, curiosity got the best of her, and she decided to call her mother to ask her why she did this. Her mother, who wasn't sure either, stated she had learned that from her own mother. So the cycle proceeded and she called her mother. In response to her daughter's inquiry the mother said, "I cut off the ends because I never owned a pan big enough to hold the entire ham!"

How often we in the church go about with our man-made doctrines and philosophies because it is what generation after generation has done all along! The sad statistics bear out, however, that this will stunt our spiritual growth—because there is no real power in our methods!

You cannot manufacture an anointing, nor do you have to. If you are a child of God, the Spirit of the Lord is upon you and He has anointed you!

Marked in the Year of God's Favor

Today is the day of the favor of the Lord in your life. You have been marked for your miracle, but Satan desires to stop you any way he can. The Bible says, however, to begin to walk in His supernatural favor and anointing, you must proclaim that not only is this your Year of Jubilee, but also this is your day of Jubilee.

Your Jubilee is not depicted by a day on the calendar, but rather, the very moment you realize that the God in Christ has become the Christ in you and you know who you are in Him!

Tomorrow is but a dream, and yesterday is but a memory, but right now—today—the Bible declares, is the day of salvation; now is the appointed time. (2 Corinthians 6:2)

Today, it is your time . . . for your thing . . . from your God, because it is God's time for His thing from you!!!

The Psalmist said it so well when speaking of the release of the children of Israel from Egyptian bondage:

When the Lord brought back the captives to Zion, we were like those who dream. [It seemed so unreal!] Turn to freedom our captivity and restore our

55

fortunes, O Lord, as the streams in the south. He who goes forth bearing seed and weeping shall doubtless come again with rejoicing, bringing his sheaves with him" (Psalm 126:1,4,6, TMB).

The man or woman who comes to God in the power of the anointing will not leave His presence empty handed! They will leave with a greater miracle harvest than was in their hand! Today, you are anointed and marked for a miracle!

Chapter 5

A Perpetual Power

After the Spirit of the Lord descended upon Jesus, like a dove, He was anointed, with a Jubilee Anointing, to go forth in the power of the Spirit to heal and deliver all who were in need.

A great physician knows that a touch can communicate so much. The will to live can be transmitted to a terminally ill patient who has lost all hope of living. It can calm the cries of parents frantic over an injured child.

The hand is a vital member of the body. When the eyes fail, the hand serves as a substitute. When the voice is silent, one touch can speak volumes to whomever it reaches. A touch is compassionate and yet authoritative.

In Luke chapter 5 we see what just one touch from our Great Physician, Jesus, can do for a desperate and dying, man. Verses 12,13 say,

And it came to pass, when he [Jesus] was in a certain city, behold a man full of leprosy: who seeing Jesus fell on his face, and besought him, saying, Lord, if thou wilt, thou canst make me clean. And he put forth his hand, and touched him, saying, I will: be thou clean. And immediately the leprosy departed from him.

This leper had every right to give up all claims to his healing. Why would the Anointed One consider touching him? Every part of his body was infected with this terrible disease. He was a detestable sight to those around him and devastated by his life of exile. By law he was destined to be separated from society.

At night he was herded like an animal, with others who had similar afflictions, to the outskirts of Jerusalem . . . to a place called Sheol. It was so named because it was what we commonly know as the city dump. It was the habitat of scavengers and sordid characters. It was the home of every rank smell and had the stench of burning refuge.

He was banished by disease and shunned by sickness. He had been detained by death itself. His heart's desire was to be touched and to touch. His only ray of hope was a divine intervention of God Himself.

But I believe that something within him said, "Cast not away therefore your confidence, which hath great recompence of reward" (Hebrews 10:35). He believed this was his Year of Jubilee. He believed he was marked for a miracle. So upon seeing Jesus he cried out to him, "Will you make me clean?"

Jesus did not send an intern to deal with this leper. He did not refer him to His disciples for treatment. His healing was not postponed because of the leper's place or position in society. Jesus is no respecter of persons, and he ministers to all alike.

The attitude of Jesus toward this man meant everything. He must have wondered, will He wince when He feels my putrefying, seeping sores? This leper surely sensed the Great Physician's true feelings in His touch—a response of great compassion.

What relief and excitement this man must have felt, for no one had touched him in so long. Through the touch of Jesus' hand, virtue flowed and drove out every sign of that sickening disease. He was no longer prisoner to a life of pain.

The effects of his healing reached beyond the boundaries of this leper's everyday life. Verse 15 of Luke chapter 5 says, "But so much the more went there a fame abroad of him: and great multitudes came together to hear, and to be healed by him of their infirmities."

The Bible records another story of when Jesus was on his way to minister to Jairus' daughter. But on His way, a woman pressed through the crowd. The Gospel of Mark, chapter 5 records these words, "When she had heard of Jesus, came in the press behind, and touched his garment. For she said, If I may touch but his clothes, I shall be whole."

What was the first thing she did? She heard Jesus was in town. This woman had possibly heard the stories of the multitudes Jesus had healed from town to town. Perhaps she heard the story of blind Bartimaeus. Maybe one of her relatives shared with her the wonderful display of compassion and deliverance toward the young child who often cast himself into the fire. Something so stirred her to the very depths of her spirit to believe this man, the carpenter's Son could heal her, also.

Secondly, she spoke to herself. Faith will cause you to talk to yourself. There are two hinges of faith found in Romans 10:10 which says, "For with **the heart** man believeth unto righteousness; and with **the mouth** confession is made unto salvation."

She then touched the hem of His garment. The word touch here is the Greek word **"hepto,"** or to take hold of. Like Jacob wrestling with the angel at the brook at Jabbock all night, this woman grabbed hold of Jesus with "pit bull" faith.

Fourth, she felt healing come in and sickness go out! Once she touched the hem of Jesus' garment she was immediately set free! How wonderful one touch can be! Many were in the crowd that day and thronged Him. They were familiar with the outward signs of a Carpenter whose face was weather beaten and whose hands were calloused. But this woman grasped hold of the Anointed One and His anointing.

Human curiosity and human interest pressed at Jesus through the crowd. But the faith of this woman latched onto the yoke-destroying, burden-removing anointing power of the Son of God!

John 3:34 records these words, "For he whom God hath sent speaketh the words of God: for God giveth not the Spirit by measure unto him."

Jesus has the Jubilee Anointing without measure. It does not matter what your need is. His anointing is not limited and His power is perpetual. He has come to meet you at the point of your greatest need!

Handkerchiefs & Aprons

The anointing of God is tangible and can be transferred. If you were to put oil on a cloth, it would soak in. The Holy Ghost anointing is like that oil.

In the Book of Acts 19:11,12 we find, "And God wrought special miracles by the hands of Paul: So that from his body were brought unto the sick handkerchiefs or aprons, and the diseases departed from them, and the evil spirits went out of them."

When the people would take the cloths from Paul and lay them upon those who were oppressed or those who were bound, the anointing which had saturated that material would destroy the yoke upon those in need.

One day I was with my pastor, Dr. Lester Sumrall, on the campus of Oral Roberts University in Tulsa, Oklahoma during a believers' meeting. We were seated next to a curtain and enjoying the service with approximately 8,000 other people. Suddenly, Dr. Sumrall put his hand on his belly and said, "Do you feel that?" At that moment something began to stir on the inside of me and I said, "Yes, I do."

Dr. Sumrall said, "I have known that anointing for nearly 50 years. It is the healing anointing. Miracles are going to transpire in this building. It is the anointing which is upon Oral Roberts. He is in the building."

At that moment, and with no knowledge that he was supposed to be there, Dr. Oral Roberts walked right in front of us, praying in the Holy Ghost.

He proceeded to the platform, interrupted the service and said, "The creative miracle-working power of God is here. It is time for you to be healed."

The power of God began to sweep through the auditorium, and hundreds of people were completely healed all over the building! This is the kind of touch hurting humanity needs! They need a Jubilee Anointing to save, heal and deliver them!

Another wonderful example of the tangible anointing of God in action can be found in Acts 5:12-15:

> And by the hands of the apostles were many signs and wonders wrought among the people; (and they were all with one accord in Solomon's porch.

> And of the rest durst no man join himself to them: but the people magnified them. And believers were the more added to the Lord, multitudes both of men and women.)

> Insomuch that they brought forth the sick into the streets, and laid them on beds and couches, that at the least the shadow of Peter passing by might overshadow some of them.

Not only did the tangible anointing fall during the days of the apostles, but also it is falling throughout the church today.

Several years ago there was a little girl in our congregation who was dying of an incurable disease. Her parents had spoken to my wife, Joni, and asked if I could pray over one of her bed sheets. They were then going to put it on her bed so she could sleep on it.

I took that bed sheet and wrapped it around my shoulders and preached an entire service, then I gave it back to the mother. Within a week that baby was up, running around and talking! The anointing is tangible!

Today is the acceptable time. Today is your time! What transpired in the book of Acts will look like a Sunday school picnic compared to what is going to happen when we begin to realize we are anointed with a Jubilee Anointing. We are marked for miracles!

The Resurrection Anointing

There is an anointing you and I can experience, the anointing of resurrection, which walked into the borrowed tomb of Joseph of Arimathea and raised the three-day dead body of the Prince of God. Paul described it this way in the book of Philippians:

> But what things were gain to me, those I counted loss for Christ. Yea doubtless, and I count all things but loss for the excellency of the knowledge of Christ Jesus my Lord: for whom I have suffered the loss of

all things, and do count them but dung, that I may win Christ,

And be found in him, not having mine own righteousness, which is of the law, but that which is through the faith of Christ, the righteousness which is of God by faith:

That I may know him, and the power of his resurrection, and the fellowship of his sufferings, being made conformable unto his death; if by any means I might attain unto the resurrection of the dead (3:7-11).

The anointing of resurrection is one of the greatest anointings available to the body of Christ in the Year of Jubilee. This is because it reaches all the way to the last foe, Death, who is cloaked in blackness and sitting upon a throne of skull and bones.

It was into a scene of death that Jesus walked, in John chapter 11, where the Bible records these words:

Now Bethany was nigh unto Jerusalem, about fifteen furlongs off: and many of the Jews came to Martha and Mary, to comfort them concerning their brother.

Then Martha, as soon as she heard that Jesus was coming, went and met him: but Mary sat still in the house. Then said Martha unto Jesus, Lord, if thou hadst been here, my brother had not died. But I know, that even now, whatsoever thou wilt ask of God, God will give it thee.

Jesus saith unto her, Thy brother shall rise again. Martha saith unto him, I know that he shall rise again in the resurrection at the last day (vv. 18-24).

Did you notice what Martha said? She said, "I know he will rise again at the last day." She was looking toward the future and not expecting a miracle then.

That is how so many view things in the body of Christ. I call it the "someday syndrome." It is more captivating than the twilight zone. The people who live there are always looking for something down the road. The mountain of their problem has eclipsed the radiance of God's power. But Jesus came to declare Jubilee today! Now is the appointed time!

Picture Jesus turning His eyes to Martha and fastening His gaze upon her as if to say, "I am the resurrection, and the life: he that believeth in me, though he were dead, yet shall he live" (vs. 25).

This is the apex of our hope—Christ arose. This is the crown jewel of our faith in God. Without the resurrection, Jesus could be cast in the same league as Buddha, Mohammed and Krishna—a sorry spectacle over which the angels of glory would weep. The validation of every claim Jesus of Nazareth ever made and the unanswerable demonstration of the most profound fact concerning His godship is this: He is not here. He is risen as He said.

Once you find the anointing of the resurrection, it does not matter where death lurks! It must bow its knee, and resurrection power will make that which was dead in your life to live again!

Christ—the Jubilee Anointing—in You

There is something at work within you. There is something producing motion against satanic resistance in your life. It is the Jubilee Anointing.

2 Corinthians 4:7 says, "But we have this treasure in earthen vessels, that the excellency of the power may be of God, and not of us."

What is that treasure? It is the Holy Ghost. The Holy Ghost is alive on the inside of you now, and He is bigger than you. Not only is He bigger than you, but He is also bigger than all your problems. He is bigger than any mountain that you can or cannot see.

John 7:38 says, "He that believeth on me, as the scripture hath said, out of his belly shall flow rivers of living water."

Your spirit becomes the generator that takes the Word of God and changes it into the fuel the Holy Ghost uses to produce the anointing in your life. It becomes your life source.

Another example of this life source can be found in Genesis chapter 26. Isaac had made plans to go to Egypt because of a terrible famine that had broken out in the land. But the Lord of Hosts spoke to him and said,

> Go not down into Egypt; dwell in the land which I shall tell thee of: Sojourn in this land, and I will be with thee, and will bless thee; for unto thee, and unto thy seed, I will give all these countries, and I will perform the oath which I sware unto Abraham thy father (vv. 2,3).

The Bible then records that Isaac pitched his tent in the valley of Gerar. While there, he found great favor with Abimelech, King of the Philistines, and he began to dig the wells which this very group of people had stopped up. When he began to dig, he found a well of "springing" water. The Hebrew word for *springing* in this passage actually means *living*.

Isaac had such favor that those from without the covenant were not able to stop the life source of God from flowing in his life. This is the way it is with the devil. When you walk in the Jubilee Anointing God has placed in your life, the adversary is unable to get to the source of that anointing on the inside of you!

But notice what happened next. The herdsman of Gerar strove with Isaac over the water but was unable to overcome him there!

Proverbs 4:23 admonishes us to, "Keep thy heart with all diligence; for out of it are the issues of life," because the devil will try to steal your fountain of power. Satan will try to stop up your well but the Spirit of the Lord will raise up a standard against him! (Isaiah 59:19)

There is an anointing on the inside of you. The same Spirit whom Jesus spoke of when He stood up in the synagogue to read from the Book of Isaiah and announced, "The Spirit of the Lord is upon me because he has anointed me," is the same Spirit which dwells in you.

This Spirit is not some third watered-down version of Jesus, nor is He a facsimile thereof. Rather, He is the mighty third Person of the Trinity which takes up residence on the inside of you. It is this same Spirit who enables you to stand in the face of defeat and adversity, when trouble is all around and closing in. It is this same Spirit which will call your lost loved ones back to God. It is this same Spirit which will drive sickness out of your body. You have the Spirit of the living God dwelling on the inside of you!

Romans 8:11 says, "But if the Spirit of him that raised up Jesus from the dead dwell in you, he that raised up Christ from the dead shall also quicken your mortal bodies by his Spirit that dwelleth in you."

The Holy Spirit within you carries with Him an anointing . . . a Jubilee Anointing . . . to mark you for the miracle you need in your life.

Maybe you don't feel like the Holy Spirit is resident in you now. Perhaps you have never understood what it means to allow the life force of God to reside in you through the baptism of the Holy Spirit, and walk in the Jubilee Anointing. Right in the middle of reading this book you can, by praying this simple prayer:

Heavenly Father, I believe your Word which says you would not leave me comfortless, but give unto me the Comforter in the person of the Holy Spirit. I ask you now to baptize me in the Holy Spirit and infuse me with power beyond myself.

Give me power to stand against the attacks of the devil and power to be a witness of your mighty acts, bearing your name in all that I say and do. I receive this power from on high now.

I receive the Jubilee Anointing in my life, as a result of this fresh baptism of fire and power, to liberate the captives, heal the brokenhearted and release all who are oppressed. I thank you for it, Lord, in the precious name of Jesus. Amen.

Chapter 6

Anointed for Service

Huddled in a small room rented over a crowded street corner, 120 people stood silently waiting for the promise. For 50 days they had anticipated the arrival of this day. During this time they had ample opportunity to quit, question and doubt the existence of this perpetual power pledged to them. But patiently they prayed, fasted and hoped against hope that their Master's words would prevail when He commanded them to go to Jerusalem and "wait for the promise of the Father which ye have heard from me."

The promise? "But ye shall receive power, after that the Holy Ghost is come upon you: and ye shall be witnesses unto me both in Jerusalem, and in all Judea, and in Samaria, and unto the uttermost part of the earth" (Acts 1:8).

After this arresting announcement, they watched as their only hope ascended into the heights of heaven in the last great earthly display of His glory.

Among those gathered in this room was a fisherman who thrice forsook the Lord, as he denied not only knowing the Messiah, but also ever speaking to Him. Two others were there who, only weeks earlier when passing this Carpenter's Son on the road to Emmaus, did not even recognize Him. Their hope was clouded by the controversy surrounding His crucifixion. This motley group, at best, was assembled of those who were anemic in faith, and who had little hope in their future, except for the last words of their King.

Now they stood waiting, watching and wondering for a sign . . . any sign.

However, all at once as lightning struck through a dark clouded sky, the Bible records, "And when the day of Pentecost was fully come, they were all with one accord in one place. And suddenly there came a sound from heaven as of a rushing mighty wind, and it filled all the house where they were sitting. And there appeared unto them cloven tongues like as of fire, and it sat upon each of them. And they were all filled with the Holy Ghost, and began to speak with other tongues, as the Spirit gave them utterance" (Acts 2:1-4).

A Domain for Demonstration

Peter—the same self-centered man who denied the Lord three times—received an anointing of the Holy Ghost on that appointed day. Imparted to him was an unfathomable energy that did for him what a phone booth did for Clark Kent—it changed him into another human being.

Instead of seeking safety in the shadows, Peter stood undauntedly before an audience of 5,000 men and preached the first Pentecostal message of the infant New Testament church. When questioned about the unusual display of "cloven tongues of fire," He commanded the crowd with this piercing proclamation:

> For these are not drunken, as ye suppose, seeing it is but the third hour of the day. But this is that which was spoken by the prophet Joel;

> And it shall come to pass in the last days, saith God, I will pour out of my Spirit upon all flesh: and your sons and your daughters shall prophesy, and your young men shall see visions, and your old men shall dream dreams: And on my servants and on my handmaidens I will pour out in those days of my Spirit; and they shall prophesy:

> And I will shew wonders in heaven above, and signs in the earth beneath; blood, and fire, and vapour of smoke: The sun shall be turned into darkness, and the moon into blood, before that great and notable day of the Lord come: and it shall come to pass, that whosoever shall call on the name of the Lord shall be saved (Acts 2:15-21).

Certain Christians

Acts 12:1-3 bears record, "Now about that time Herod the king stretched forth his hands to vex certain of the church. And he killed James the brother of John with the sword. And because he saw it pleased the Jews, he proceeded further to take Peter also. (Then were the days of unleavened bread.)"

Let me set the stage for you. Herod had unleashed an all-out assault against the church, and he did it during one of the most holy times. This passage states all of the havoc he raised was during the week of unleavened bread. This was also the Day of Atonement, or the same time as Jubilee.

I want you to take special notice of the word "certain" in verse one. The word certain denotes a specific segment of the church. I like to think of it this way: Herod came against the Davids, Samuels and Daniels of the church, or those he felt were the biggest threats to his empire.

The word "vex" translates "to afflict, torment, harass or cause terrible suffering." Maybe you feel as though Jubilee has passed you by, but I want to encourage you to take heart! The very fact you are tormented by trials, tribulation and troubles is a very good indicator you are right in the midst of Jubilee!

When you walk in the Jubilee Anointing, not only will you experience the blessing and favor of the Lord, but also you will encounter the Herods who desire to take you out!

There's a song I love to sing which says, "How beautiful heaven must be, sweet home of the happy and free!"

When I get to heaven and the roll is called, it really makes no difference to me where my name falls on the list. I just want to know that my name is there, written by the blood of the Lamb. There is another list, however, I want

74

to be on, and that is the devil's hit list! I want to be a devil tormentor!

Peter was a devil tormentor. That is why Herod sought to lock him away in prison! As I shared with you earlier, Luke's Gospel declares, "And the Lord said, Simon, Simon, behold, Satan hath desired to have you, that he may sift you as wheat: But I have prayed for thee, that thy faith fail not: and when thou art converted, strengthen thy brethren" (Luke 22:31,32).

The "desire" the devil referred to here means, "heavy passionate breathing and refusing everything else that he might win you." The devil was out to stop Peter at any cost, because he had a revelation of who Jesus was. When you get a revelation of Him, you become a target not only of the favor of God, but also the attacks of the devil.

How do you combat the enemy's attack? Ephesians 6:11-13 says we must,

> Put on the whole armour of God, that ye may be able to stand against the wiles of the devil. For we wrestle not against flesh and blood, but against principalities, against powers, against the rulers of the darkness of this world, against spiritual wickedness in high places.
>
> Wherefore take unto you the whole armour of God, that ye may be able to withstand in the evil day, and having done all, to stand.

Jesus also offered these comforting words, "I am praying for you, Peter, that your faith doesn't fail." Jesus is praying for you also, and He never prayed the prayer that His Father did not answer!

It was this same Peter who was with John when he came upon a lame man (Acts 3:1-8):

Now Peter and John went up together into the temple at the hour of prayer, being the ninth hour. And a certain man lame from his mother's womb was carried, whom they laid daily at the gate of the temple which is called Beautiful, to ask alms of them that entered into the temple; who seeing Peter and John about to go into the temple asked an alms.

And Peter, fastening his eyes upon him with John, said, Look on us. And he gave heed unto them, expecting to receive something of them.

Then Peter said, Silver and gold have I none; but such as I have give I thee: In the name of Jesus Christ of Nazareth rise up and walk.

And he took him by the right hand, and lifted him up: and immediately his feet and ankle bones received strength. And he leaping up stood, and walked, and entered with them into the temple, walking, and leaping, and praising God.

The Bible calls this man a "certain" lame man. I like to compare this man with Mephibosheth, Jonathan's son and Saul's grandson. Mephibosheth was a cripple, but he was heir to his father's throne. The only problem was that he didn't know he was rich all along. Mephibosheth was an heir apparent.

Romans 8:15,16 states it this way, "For ye have not received the spirit of bondage again to fear; but ye have received the Spirit of adoption, whereby we cry, Abba, Father. The Spirit itself beareth witness with our spirit, that we are the children of God."

The Lord went to the adoption agency just to get to you. You may not look like much, but you caught His eye; and He didn't want to go home without you! You are His favorite!

Psalm 16:13,14 in The Message Bible says, "My choice is you, God, first and only. And now I find I'm your choice! You set me up with a house and yard, and then you made me your heir!"

The lame man was sought out by God. Before he ever had an opportunity to receive Jesus as his Savior, the Lord had targeted him for blessing.

There are many, many accounts recorded in history of men and women who have been knocked broadside by the adversary in his futile attempt to stop them from fulfilling their destiny in God.

Oral Roberts was afflicted with tuberculosis and given no hope. My pastor, Dr. Lester Sumrall, was stricken with tuberculosis as well. The doctor even signed his death certificate while he was living, claiming he would be dead by morning anyway.

My own mother was hit by a heart attack at the age of 29, which fractured her heart in several places. She was the youngest woman to ever suffer such an attack of this magnitude. My wife, Joni, was thrown off a cliff at the age of 14. But may I remind you, if you have been hit by the devil, it is a great indication that your target is in place!

Like Mephibosheth and the man at the gate Beautiful, you may feel as though God put you in the place you are in just for the crumbs, BUT that is not all your life is worth! He may just use the crumbs to maneuver and strategically locate you into a better position. In eternity past, the Lord of Hosts laid out the mechanism whereby you would meet your miracle!

The lame man met his healing, and you will meet your breakthrough as well!

Signs and Wonders

Several years ago a dear friend of mine decided to set aside a time of prayer to seek the face of the Lord. During the days and weeks that ensued, she diligently fasted and prayed before God, desperately seeking the anointing. One day as she was crawling through the house, weeping and crying in the presence of the Lord, she came into the restroom. With tears streaming down her face and her hands lifted in reverent worship, she lay prostrate over the toilet and said, "Oh, God, I want the anointing! Oh, Jesus, I need the anointing!"

At that very instant the Holy Spirit gently and tenderly spoke into the depths of her heart, "The toilet doesn't need a healing!"

The hour you and I are living in is a day of signs and wonders. It is imperative to show forth the power of God through the anointing resident within our lives. Isaiah 8:18 proclaims, "Behold, I and the children whom the Lord hath given me are for signs and for wonders in Israel from the Lord of hosts, which dwelleth in mount Zion."

Jesus promised, "I will pray the Father, and he shall give you another Comforter, that he may abide with you for ever; even the Spirit of truth; whom the world cannot receive, because it seeth him not, neither knoweth him: but ye know him; for he dwelleth with you, and shall be in you" (John 14:16,17).

2 Corinthians 4:7 declares, "But we have this treasure in earthen vessels, that the excellency of the **power** may be of God, and not of us." The power we possess is referred to as "dunamis" in the Greek or "a propelling energy."

Ephesians 3:20 declares, "Now unto him that is able to do exceeding abundantly above all that we ask or think, according to the power that worketh in us."

The Holy Spirit is at work throughout the body of Christ to confirm His Word. He is removing all doubt by performing indisputable acts of authority through a mighty display of His power!

A Signpost for God's Power

God is looking for a people within a people, a church within a church, a city within a city, a nation within a nation who will not accept the status quo of religion. He is seeking those who will not settle for anything less than a revelation of Jesus Christ, the Anointed One.

The Jubilee Anointing the Lord has marked us with is not for our own self-gratification, but rather, it is to meet the needs of lost and hurting people who are helpless and hopeless without God. It is our responsibility to take the person of the Messiah to our city, nation and the world.

The world does not want another dead, cold sect which propagates the dead rigors of religion. They do not crave the cadencing creeds of creation. Man-made doctrines cannot mask the real manifestation of miracles empty hearts yearn for.

What this generation needs is a display of Jesus' anointing that outstrips human ability and gives hope beyond the scope of human limitation. They are in search of a force that puts them in contact with the reality of a resurrected Christ who broke the bands of wickedness and slew death itself and gives power unto as many as will call upon the name of Jesus.

The earth-shaking revival this world seeks will only come as we reveal the Christ within us who has called us and anointed us for such a time as this.

In order to display the Jubilee Anointing, we must recognize that greater is He who is in us than He who is in the world (1 John 4:4). Philippians 2:13-15 says, "For it is

God which worketh in you both to will and to do of his good pleasure. Do all things without murmurings and disputings: That ye may be blameless and harmless, the sons of God, without rebuke, in the midst of a crooked and perverse nation, among whom ye shine as lights in the world."

In 2 Kings 2 this is what the Israelites suffered from. They had trees, they had water they had seed but their trees were miscarrying. They weren't bearing any fruit; there was something missing. The Bible goes on to reveal that the waters were naught.

We are missing something in the body of Christ today and the Book of Acts reveals the ingredient we are missing is a revelation of Jesus. Coupled with the Holy Ghost, a revelation of the King of kings and Lord of lords will cause us to be a mighty army raised up to display the message of Jesus.

Through the power of the Holy Ghost, we are enabled to do what we cannot do. Charles Spurgeon once said, "Apart from the Spirit of God we can do nothing." We do not need more mechanical irrigation; we need divine intervention.

The Great Commission

With hands lifted and hearts raised it is our time to go forth with the Jubilee Anointing resident deep within our spiritual belly to proclaim the acceptable year of the Lord. Proclaim it not only in our personal lives and families, but also to all those who are held in bondage to sin, sickness and disease. From the nail-pierced hands of the Anointed One, we have received our marching orders:

Go ye into all the world, and preach the gospel to every creature. He that believeth and is baptized shall be saved; but he that believeth not shall be damned.

And these signs shall follow them that believe; In my name shall they cast out devils; they shall speak with new tongues; They shall take up serpents; and if they drink any deadly thing, it shall not hurt them; they shall lay hands on the sick, and they shall recover.

So then after the Lord had spoken unto them, he was received up into heaven, and sat on the right hand of God. And they went forth, and preached every where, the Lord working with them, and confirming the word with signs following. Amen (Mark 16:15-20).

We are to do the works that Jesus did and even "greater works" according to John 14:12, because He went to be with the Father and gave a tag team handoff to the Holy Ghost.

We have the answer for every human need. For those sick in body, there is a balm in Gilead. For those who mourn, we pour out the oil of gladness. For those held captive with hands chained and feet fettered to the enticement of sin, we offer the Anointed Messiah.

The question now is, will we go and proclaim the message, "It is finished! Today is the year of the favor of the Lord!"

In this Year of Jubilee, God has already made the provision for us to possess our promised land. For in His heart He knew there would be a people who would not settle for a life of low-living, sight-walking and tame-vision. He, through the telescope of time, saw a remnant people who would take Him at His Word .

The year of the favor of our Lord has been proclaimed. The day of the vengeance of our God has been published. And, Jesus is leading us back to the boundary of that beautiful garden where the first Adam forfeited our inheritance.

Our King of kings and Lord of lords has arrived to pronounce prosperity to the poor. He has ascended to salvage us from a slave mentality. He has appeared to proclaim liberty to those who are bruised by suffering, crushed by sorrow and broken down by calamity.

He is coaxing us to the edge of eternity and anointing our eyes to gaze beyond the horizon of our human limitations and to believe for every desire to be fulfilled in this Dream Year.

As the message is heralded through the sound of Jubilee, the miracle they will see is an empty garden tomb. Jesus is no longer there. He is risen and has come to proclaim the year of Jubilee.

We have been painted and purposely marked with the fragrance to attract the favor and blessing of God. And, if you will listen closely, you can almost hear Jesus say, "This is My year to act!"

Listen to the sound of the shofar as our High Priest puts it to His lips and begins to noise abroad release, restitution and return of our deliverance and may our hearts cry out in response, "I am anointed, Lord! Here am I! Send me!"

Conclusion

Don't Change the Sheets!

My pastor, mentor and friend, Dr. Lester Sumrall, shared with me a story of Smith Wigglesworth ministering in a small town. While in that town he stayed in the home of a precious saint of God whose husband was not saved. The meetings progressed, the Holy Spirit moved and still her husband was lost without God. One day, however, the Lord prompted Brother Wigglesworth that his time there was finished—it was time to move on.

This precious lady cried out to Brother Wigglesworth, "Please don't leave, for my husband is not yet saved!" But while he stayed in her home, he had slept in their bed. So on his way out the door he yelled back to her, "Just don't change the sheets!"

That night as she and her husband were settling down in bed for the evening, something came upon him! The convicting power of the Holy Ghost began to overcome him. He began breaking out in a sweat and breathing heavily. He started to fan himself as if trying to extinguish the very flames of hell, when all of a sudden he cried out as if in pain. His wife looked at him and said nonchalantly, "What is wrong?"

He cried out all the more, "Woman! I feel like I am quickly sinking into the bowels of eternal fire and damnation, and I don't know what is going on!" He screamed out, "What have you done?" She responded, "Brother Wigglesworth slept here and told me if I wanted to see you saved, that I was not to change the sheets!" That very night her husband bowed at the base of his bed and gave his life to Jesus!

I want to proclaim, *"Don't change the sheets!"*

You may say, "Brother Rod, I have been standing for so long for my miracle. I have fasted and prayed and believed and still have not received my breakthrough!" Let me remind you this is your day of the favor of the Lord! This is the year of Jubilee when everything goes back to God! Everything in your life—your body, your finances, your mind, your children, your husband, your wife, your family—they all go back to God! *"Don't change the sheets!"* Get as close to the anointing of God as you can!

When the world wants you to give up on your dream, *"Don't change the sheets!"* When your friends say your child will never be saved, *"Don't change the sheets!"* When the doctor looks at you and says you have to die and cannot live, *"Don't change the sheets!"* When your heart feels as if it has been shattered into a million pieces and the pain of your past eclipses your hope for a better day, *"Don't change the sheets!"*

David said of Jehovah God in Psalm 20:6, "Now know I that the Lord saveth his anointed; he will hear him from his holy heaven with the saving strength of his right hand."

There is a balm, or an anointing, in Gilead. The Anointed One has come to **anoint you** with joy and hope. Jesus, the Messiah, your Rock of Ages, your Fortress, your Strength and your Friend has come to put upon you the garment or mantel of praise.

Praise is translated as favor and is for the spirit of heaviness or hopelessness. When all seems lost and future anticipation of change is gone, there is an anchor of hope in Jesus!

Psalm 92:10 proclaims, "But my horn you have exalted like that of a wild ox; I am anointed with fresh oil" (AMP).

There is an anointing upon you! You don't need more inspiration; you don't need more knowledge that touches the head and misses the heart! You need the power from on high! You need the oil of the Holy Spirit to purify and heal! You need the anointing!

The Jubilee Anointing Prayer

You have come to the Kingdom of God for such a time as this. This is your hour and this is your day. This is your opportunity for divine destiny to cause the Word of God to be fulfilled, "These that have turned the world upside down are come hither also" (Acts 17:6).

So I bless you now. I bless you beyond the capacity of human limitation. I dig deep within me to the anointing which resides forever, and I release that anointing upon you from the crown of your head to the soles of your feet.

You have spent your last ordinary moment.

I command your perception of the world to be seen through the focus of the blood of the Cross of Christ. I mark you now by that cross. Even as our Savior bears those marks, so you are marked by God!

I mark you with the anointing of God. You will see as God sees and hear as God hears.

You will receive an insatiable hunger and desire for the courts of your God, and nothing of this earth will satisfy your craving. I speak within you a chasm that can only be filled by the flooding presence of the Holy Ghost.

May you be released from the fear of your past, the fear of your present and the fear of your future. May you know Jesus as no person has ever known Him, and may everywhere you go the witness of the people declare, "The anointed people of God are among us."

Now it is time to press forward toward the mark of the high calling and to forget those things which are behind. May this be your prayer:

"The Spirit of the Lord [is] upon Me, because He has **anointed** Me [the Anointed One, the Messiah] to preach the good news (the Gospel) to the poor; He has sent Me to announce release to the captives and recovery of sight to the blind, to send forth as delivered those who are oppressed [who are downtrodden, bruised, crushed, and broken down by calamity], to proclaim the accepted and acceptable year of the Lord [the day when salvation and the free favors of God profusely abound]" (Luke 4:18, 19 AMP)

Anointing Scriptures

And it shall come to pass, if ye shall hearken diligently unto my commandments which I command you this day, to love the Lord your God, and to serve him with all your heart and with all your soul, that I will give you the rain of your land in his due season, the first rain and the latter rain, that thou mayest gather in thy corn, and thy wine, and thine oil (Deuteronomy 11:13,14).

He will keep the feet of his saints, and the wicked shall be silent in darkness; for by strength shall no man prevail. The adversaries of the Lord shall be broken to pieces; out of heaven shall he thunder upon them: the Lord shall judge the ends of the earth; and he shall give strength unto his king, and exalt the horn of his anointed (1 Samuel 2:9,10).

And Samuel said unto Jesse, Are here all thy children? And he said, There remaineth yet the youngest, and, behold, he keepeth the sheep. And Samuel said unto Jesse, Send and fetch him: for we will not sit down till he come hither. And he sent, and brought him in. Now he was ruddy, and withal of a beautiful countenance, and goodly to look to. And the Lord said, Arise, anoint him: for this is he. Then Samuel took the horn of oil, and anointed him in the midst of his brethren: and the Spirit of the Lord came upon David from that day forward. So Samuel rose up, and went to Ramah (1 Samuel 16:11-13).

And let Zadok the priest and Nathan the prophet anoint him there king over Israel: and blow ye with the trumpet, and say, God save king Solomon (1 Kings 1:34).

Touch not mine anointed, and do my prophets no harm (1 Chronicles 16:22).

Now know I that the Lord saveth his anointed; he will hear him from his holy heaven with the saving strength of his right hand (Psalm 20:6).

Thou preparest a table before me in the presence of mine enemies: thou anointest my head with oil; my cup runneth over (Psalm 23:5).

The Lord is my strength and my shield; my heart trusted in him, and I am helped: therefore my heart greatly rejoiceth; and with my song will I praise him. The Lord is their strength, and he is the saving strength of his anointed (Psalm 28:7,8).

Thou lovest righteousness, and hatest wickedness: therefore God, thy God, hath anointed thee with the oil of gladness above thy fellows (Psalm 45:7).

There is a river, the streams whereof shall make glad the city of God, the holy place of the tabernacles of the most High (Psalm 46:4).

Behold, O God our shield, and look upon the face of thine anointed (Psalm 84:9).

But my horn shalt thou exalt like the horn of an unicorn: I shall be anointed with fresh oil (Psalm 92:10).

There is treasure to be desired and oil in the dwelling of the wise; but a foolish man spendeth it up (Proverbs 21:20).

And it shall come to pass in that day, that his burden shall be taken away from off thy shoulder, and his yoke from off thy neck, and the yoke shall be destroyed because of the anointing (Isaiah 10:27).

The Spirit of the Lord God is upon me; because the Lord hath anointed me to preach good tidings unto the meek; he hath sent me to bind up the brokenhearted, to proclaim liberty to the captives, and the opening of the prison to them that are bound; to proclaim the acceptable year of the Lord, and the day of vengeance of our God; to comfort all that mourn; to appoint unto them that mourn in Zion, to give unto them beauty for ashes, the oil of joy for mourning, the garment of praise for the spirit of heaviness; that they might be called trees of righteousness, the planting of the Lord, that he might be glorified (Isaiah 61:1-3).

Then shall we know . . . his going forth is prepared as the morning; and he shall come unto us as the rain, as the latter and former rain unto the earth (Hosea 6:3).

Yea, the Lord will answer and say unto his people, Behold, I will send you corn, and wine, and oil, and ye shall be satisfied therewith: and I will no more make you a reproach among the heathen (Joel 2:19).

Be glad then, ye children of Zion, and rejoice in the Lord your God: for he hath given you the former rain moderately, and he will cause to come down for you the rain, the former rain, and the latter rain in the first month. And the floors shall be full of wheat, and the fats shall overflow with wine and oil. And I will restore to you the years that the locust hath eaten, the cankerworm, and the caterpillar, and the palmerworm, my great army which I sent among you. And ye shall eat in plenty, and be satisfied, and praise the name of the Lord your God, that hath dealt wondrously with you: and my people shall never be ashamed (Joel 2:23-26).

The Spirit of the Lord is upon me, because he hath anointed me to preach the gospel to the poor; he hath sent me to heal the brokenhearted, to preach deliverance to the captives, and recovering of sight to the blind, to set at liberty them that are bruised, To preach the acceptable year of the Lord (Luke 4:18,19).

He that believeth on me, as the scripture hath said, out of his belly shall flow rivers of living water (John 7:38).

But unto the Son he saith, Thy throne, O God, is for ever and ever: a sceptre of righteousness is the sceptre of thy kingdom. Thou hast loved righteousness, and hated iniquity; therefore God, even thy God, hath anointed thee with the oil of gladness above thy fellows (Hebrews 1:8,9).

Is any sick among you? let him call for the elders of the church; and let them pray over him, anointing him with oil in the name of the Lord: And the prayer of faith shall save the sick, and the Lord shall raise him up; and if he have committed sins, they shall be forgiven him (James 5:14, 15).

But ye have an unction from the Holy One, and ye know all things (1 John 2:20).

But the anointing which ye have received of him abideth in you, and ye need not that any man teach you: but as the same anointing teacheth you of all things, and is truth, and is no lie, and even as it hath taught you, ye shall abide in him (1 John 2:27).

ABOUT THE AUTHOR

Rod Parsley began his ministry as an energetic 19-year-old in the backyard of his parents' Ohio home. The fresh, "old-time gospel" approach of Parsley's delivery immediately attracted a hungry, God-seeking audience. From the 17 people who attended Parsley's first 1977 backyard meeting, the crowds rapidly grew.

Today, as the pastor of Columbus, Ohio's 5,200-seat World Harvest Church, Parsley oversees World Harvest Christian Academy, World Harvest Bible College, Bridge of Hope missions and outreach, and "Breakthrough," World Harvest Church's daily and weekly television broadcast. Parsley's message to "Raise the Standard" of spiritual intensity, moral integrity and physical purity not only extends across North America, but also spans the globe to nearly 136 nations via television and shortwave radio.

Thousands in arenas across the country and around the world experience the saving, healing and delivering message of Jesus Christ as Parsley calls people back to Bible basics.

Rod Parsley currently resides in Pickerington, Ohio, with his wife, Joni, and their two children, Ashton and Austin.

OTHER BOOKS BY
ROD PARSLEY

Backside of Calvary
Breakthrough Quotes
Ten Golden Keys Special Edition Bridge Builders' Bible
The Commanded Blessing
Covenant Blessings
Daily Breakthrough
Free at Last
God's Answer to Insufficient Funds
He Sent His Word and Healed Them
Holiness: Living Leaven Free
I'm Glad You Asked
My Promise Is the Palace
No Dry Season (best seller)
No More Crumbs (best seller)
Power From Above
Renamed and Redeemed
Repairers of the Breach
Serious Survival Strategies
Ten Golden Keys to Your Abundance
Tribulation to Triumph

For information about *Breakthrough*,
World Harvest Church or to receive a product list of the
many books and audio and video tapes
by Rod Parsley write or call:

Breakthrough
P.O. Box 32932
Columbus, Ohio 43232-0932
(614) 837-1990

For information about World Harvest Bible College,
write or call:

World Harvest Bible College
P.O. Box 32901
Columbus, Ohio 43232-0901
(614) 837-4088

If you need prayer, the *Breakthrough* prayer line is open
24 hours a day, 7 days a week.
(614) 837-3232

Visit Rod Parsley at his website address:
www.breakthrough.net

NOTES

NOTES

Recent Ministry Tools by Rod Parsley

No More Crumbs *(Best Seller)*
With vivid imagery and profound biblical insight Rod Parsley challenges you to stop settling for the crumbs of life, and to set aside your failures and forgotten dreams! The King of kings is waiting to dine with you!
   #BK 924 (Book) $20
   #TS 123 (Audio) ....4/$20

Jubilee . . .
Reaping Your Supernatural Harvest
This 5-tape series is filled with prophetic teaching and fresh revelation to help you reap your supernatural harvest in this first spiritual Year of Jubilee in nearly 2,000 years.
   #TS 122 (Audio) ....5/$25
   #VS 55 (Video) ....5/$50

The Sound Of Jubliee
Through these fourteen anointed songs and the reading of God's Word join us in the Jubilee celebration and receive a fresh revelation of Jesus—our Jubilee.
   CD 238...$12
   MA 236 ....$8
   MV 237 ....$20

The Best of Rod Parsley
Celebrating 20 years of Spirit-filled preaching of the Gospel with this anniversary collection of 20 of Rod Parsley's greatest messages on audio cassette in a handsome binder.
   #AS 03 (Audio) ....24/$50

Soaring With Eagles
As the eagle teaches her young, God teaches us to soar in His glory in the good times, while He gently carries us in our trials. These messages will teach you how to attain new heights in your relationship with your heavenly Father.
   #TS 121 (Audio) ....4/$20

No Dry Season *(Best Seller)*
Raising high God's standard of living for this final generation, *No Dry Season* equips you to experience the blessings of kingdom living and arms you to march forth restoring what has been lost.
   #BK 919 (Book) $15

Daily Breakthrough
This will be your daily guide to Holy Spirit-empowered prayer and Bible study. Each stirring message includes a prayer and Scripture. As you read and study, every day, you'll be released from your painful past and begin to experience God's promises, provision and restoration for your life.

#CDEV (Book)...$10

10 Golden Keys Special Edition
Bridge Builders' Bible
85 pages of personal instruction on becoming a Bridge Builder for hurting humanity, plus a 33 page bonus section of Rod Parsley's 10 Golden Keys To Your Abundance teaching. This high-quality, bonded-leather King James Version of the Bible will serve you and your family for years to come.

#BK 922 (Book)..$50

Final Awakening, The
This is the last act! Three powerful messages reveal the curtain on the scene of life is going up as the finale begins, and this sleeping giant called the church is beginning to stir and walk out of the blurs of indistinction and take her place for the Final Awakening.

#TS 98 (Audio)...4/$20
#VS 39 (Video)...4/$60